Dedicated To:
Sr. Kelly Grace, Sr. Lucia,
Sr. Monica Bernadette, and Sr. Odelia

Thank you for your beautiful witness and love for our community.

Written By: Abigail Gartland

I was born in Portugal near Fatima, in 1910.

When I was a little girl, I loved to play with my older brother, Francisco, and my cousin, Lucia.

Francisco, Lucia and worked together to take care of our family's animals.

I was so thankful to Jesus for my family and my life!

One day, Francisco, Lucia and I were out in our field when a very bright light appeared.

We watched the bright light, and a beautiful woman appeared to us.

She was our beautiful mother, Mary! She told us to pray the rosary each day for peace in the world.

Before Mary left us that day, she told us that she would come back and appear to us again on the 13th of every month.

I spent my days praying the rosary for peace and for the conversion of sinners

A few years later, Francisco and I both became very sick with the flu.

Mary appeared to us one night and told us that Francisco would be going to Heaven very soon.

Mary also said she would like to take me to Heaven, too, but I want to spend more time praying on Earth.

After Francisco passed away, I prayed as much as I could every single day, I was still sick and joined him, Mary and Jesus in Heaven nearly a year later.

I went to Heaven on February 20, 1920.

Do you want to be more like me?

You can celebrate my feast day with me on February 20th

I am the patron saint of sick people and kids!

I pray for you every day of your life.

St. Jacinta, pray for us!

opyright:

part: © PentoolPixie © LimeandKiwiDesigns
ensed purchased: 1/10/2024

About the Author

Abigail Gartland

I love the saints and I love my faith. The idea for sharing the stories of the saints with little ones came when my dear friends were expecting their first baby. I wanted to create something as unique and special as our friendship. Each book is dedicated to very special people and groups who have enriched my faith in different ways. I am blessed to write these stories and appreciate the unending support of my family and friends. When I am not writing, am a middle school teacher. I hope you enjoy these stories. I pray for each and every person who opens one of my books to learn more about the saints.

Abbie

www.ingramcontent.com/pod-product-compliance
Lightning Source LLC
LaVergne TN
LVHW051042070526
838201LV00067B/4888